W9-AOA-093

dabble lab

AMAZING MAGIC TRICKS

ALAKAZAM!

TRICKS FOR **VETERAN** MAGICIANS

4D™

A MAGICAL AUGMENTED
READING
EXPERIENCE

• • • BY NORM BARNHART • • •

CAPSTONE PRESS
a capstone imprint

Dabble Lab is published by
Capstone Press, A Capstone Imprint
1710 Roe Crest Drive
North Mankato, Minnesota 56003
www.mycapstone.com

Library of Congress Cataloging-in-Publication Data
Names: Barnhart, Norm, author.
Title: Alakazam! : tricks for veteran magicians : 4D a magical augmented reading experience / by Norm Barnhart.
Description: Mankato, Minnesota : Capstone Press, 2018. | Series: Dabble lab.
  Amazing magic tricks 4D | Includes bibliographical references and index. |
  Audience: Age 8-12. | Audience: Grade 4 to 6.
Identifiers: LCCN 2017035465 (print) | LCCN 2017039151 (ebook) |
  ISBN 9781543505764 (eBook PDF) | ISBN 9781543505719 (library binding)
Subjects: LCSH: Magic tricks—Juvenile literature.
Classification: LCC GV1548 (ebook) | LCC GV1548 .B35199 2018 (print) | DDC 793.8—dc23
LC record available at https://lccn.loc.gov/2017035465

. . . . . .

EDITOR:
Aaron J. Sautter

DESIGNER:
Ted Williams

PRODUCTION:
Katy LaVigne

. . . . . .

Image Credits
All photographs and video are done by Capstone Studio

Design Elements
Shutterstock: findracadabra, G.roman, javarman, popular business

Printed and bound in the USA.
010758S18

TABLE OF CONTENTS

✪ FANTASTIC MAGIC! 4

✪ THE IMPOSSIBLE COIN 6

✪ THE TRICKY LIZARD 8

✪ THE MAGIC ACE 10

✪ TOMMY, THE TRAINED PING PONG BALL 12

✪ THE NUMBER ONE FAN...................... 14

✪ THE CONFUSING COIN MYSTERY 18

✪ THE SPOOKY SPOON........................ 20

✪ THE MAGIC MATCHBOX BANK................. 22

✪ THE EGG-STRAORDINARY EGG 24

✪ THE AMAZING HEALING ROPE 26

......

GLOSSARY.................................. 30

READ MORE 31

INTERNET SITES 31

INDEX 32

FANTASTIC MAGIC!

Welcome to the world of magic! With this book you'll learn the secrets behind some amazing tricks. Magicians aren't just tricksters. They also work hard to entertain their audiences. Whether performing for a few friends or a large crowd, your main job is to make sure your audience enjoys the show. Now let's learn how to do some fantastic magic!

THE KEYS TO MAGIC

⭐ **Practice, practice, practice!** Try standing in front of a mirror while practicing with your props. Then you can see what the tricks look like to your audience.

⭐ **Keep it secret!** If you reveal the secrets of a trick, people won't be very impressed. It also ruins the trick for other magicians.

⭐ **Be entertaining!** Tell the audience jokes or stories while you do your tricks. It will keep them coming back for more.

A MAGIC SECRET – MISDIRECTION

Misdirection is an important part of magic. Magicians misdirect audiences by focusing their eyes on what they want people to look at. Then they can secretly hide an object in their pocket or magic trunk while the audience is focused on something else. With practice, you can be a master of misdirection too!

DOWNLOAD THE CAPSTONE 4D APP!

- Ask an adult to search in the Apple App Store or Google Play for "Capstone 4D".
- Click Install (Android) or Get, then Install (Apple).
- Open the app.
- Scan any of the following spreads with this icon:

When you scan a spread, you'll find fun extra stuff to go with this book!
You can also find these things on the web at
www.capstone4D.com using the password **magic.veteran**

MEET THE MAGICIAN! ⭐

Norm Barnhart is a professional comic magician who has entertained audiences for nearly 40 years. In 2007 Norm was named America's Funniest Magician by the Family Entertainers Workshop. Norm's travels have taken him across the United States and many countries around the world. He also loves to get kids excited about reading. Norm says, **"I love bringing smiles to people of all ages with magic. After reading this book, kids will love to do magic tricks too."**

THE IMPOSSIBLE COIN

Magicians have been doing coin tricks for thousands of years. This trick will really stump your audience. People won't believe their eyes when a coin disappears into thin air!

WHAT YOU NEED

* ⭐ One playing card
* ⭐ Two identical coins
* ⭐ Glue

PREPARATION

1. First, glue one coin to the face side of the playing card as shown. Then put the other coin into your pocket.

PERFORMANCE

1. Begin by telling the audience how tricky money can be. Say, "Sometimes coins disappear right out of my hand!" Then show them the card with the coin. Be sure not to tip it, or they'll see that the coin is stuck to the card.

SEE HOW IT'S DONE

2. Next, turn the card toward you as shown and pretend to dump the coin into your hand. Turning the card toward you keeps people from seeing that the coin is stuck to the card.

3. Now, close your hand and pretend to hold the coin. Then toss the card into your magic trunk and pick up your magic wand.

4. Tap your hand with the wand three times. Then open your hand to show that the coin has vanished.

5. Finally, reach into your pocket and bring out the second coin. The audience will believe it's the same coin that just vanished. They'll really wonder how the coin jumped from your hand into your pocket!

THE TRICKY LIZARD

Most reptiles aren't very fast. But this tricky lizard can zip out of sight in a split second. Your audience will have a good laugh when they see it climbing on your back!

WHAT YOU NEED

- ⭐ A poster or book showing the desert
- ⭐ A small toy lizard
- ⭐ Black thread
- ⭐ A safety pin
- ⭐ A black jacket

PREPARATION

1. First, tie one end of the thread to the safety pin and the other end to the toy lizard. Then attach the pin to the back of your shirt or jacket collar as shown.

Pin

2. Next, bring the toy lizard under your arm so the thread runs under it as shown. Then place the lizard in your chest pocket. The audience should not be able to see the thread when it's hidden against the black jacket.

Thread

SEE HOW IT'S DONE

1. Pull the toy lizard out of your pocket and show it to the audience. Tell them a story about how hard it is to keep track of the tricky reptile. Let them know it often disappears and tries to get back to its desert home.

2. Next, cover the lizard with the desert picture. As you do this, secretly drop the lizard and let it swing around to land on your back. Then pull away the picture to show that the lizard has vanished!

3. Now, pretend to look around for the tricky lizard. Where did it go? Ask the audience if they saw where it went. Finally, turn around. The audience will see the lizard hanging on your back. Act amazed and confused about how it got there. The audience will get a big laugh out of this trick!

THE MAGIC ACE

The Ace of Spades is the world's most magical card. This trick will blow your friends away when the Ace turns invisible and magically appears in your pocket!

WHAT YOU NEED

- ⭐ Two identical Ace of Spades cards
- ⭐ Seven other cards
- ⭐ Glue
- ⭐ Scissors

PREPARATION

1. First, put one Ace of Spades in your pocket or up your sleeve. Cut the second Ace in half diagonally and glue one half to another card as shown.

2. The secret to this trick is in how you hold the cards. The Ace of Spades can be seen when the cards are fanned out one way. But when the cards are turned around and fanned out again, the Ace is hidden.

1. First, tell the audience a story about the magical Ace. Say, "The Ace of Spades can turn invisible any time it wants." Next, fan the cards out so the audience can see the Ace. Ask someone if they can see the Ace of Spades. Then turn the cards over and pretend to take out an invisible card as shown.

2. Next, put down the cards and pretend to put the invisible Ace in your pocket or up your sleeve. Then, pick up the cards again. As you pick them up, be sure to turn the cards around. Keep talking to the audience so they don't notice that you turn the cards around. Now, fan out the cards again and show the audience that the Ace of Spades has disappeared!

3. Finally, reach into your pocket or sleeve and pull out the secret Ace of Spades. Show it to your audience. Ask them to give the Ace a round of applause as you pretend that it takes a bow!

SEE HOW IT'S DONE

TOMMY, THE TRAINED PING-PONG BALL

Normal ping-pong balls just bounce around a lot. But this magic ping-pong ball can do a great trick. People will be astonished when it does an amazing balancing act!

WHAT YOU NEED

- ✪ A ping-pong ball
- ✪ A magic wand
- ✪ Black thread
- ✪ Tape
- ✪ Scissors
- ✪ A table

PREPARATION

1. First, cut a piece of thread a little longer than the magic wand. Then use small pieces of tape to attach the thread to the wand on both ends. Make sure the thread stays a little loose in the middle.

PERFORMANCE

1. Start by bouncing the ping-pong ball on the table a couple of times. Tell the audience a story about the ball. Say, "Tommy looks like a normal ping-pong ball. But he is really a magic ball. He can do a fun balancing act!"

SEE HOW IT'S DONE

2. When you're ready to do the trick, hold the wand with your thumbs under the thread as shown. The thread will help balance the ball.

3. Be sure to keep the thread facing you so the audience can't see it. Now, place the ball on the wand and balance it on the thread.

4. To the audience, the ball will look like it is balancing on the wand. Gently tilt the wand up and down a little so the ball travels back and forth. The ball will seem to be doing a dangerous balancing act.

To end the trick, toss the ball up in the air, catch it, and toss it to someone in the audience. While they look at it, toss the wand into your magic trunk. Then ask the audience for a round of applause for Tommy, the tricky ping-pong ball!

THE NUMBER ONE FAN

This trick will astound any sports fan. Your audience will be stunned when you pull a big league sports star out of a hat!

WHAT YOU NEED

- A giant foam finger
- A baseball hat
- Two identical sports cards
- Five other sports cards
- Tape

PREPARATION

1. First, place a circle of tape on the back of one of the identical cards. Then tuck the secret card into the baseball hat under the rim on one side as shown. Be sure the tape faces the inside of the hat and isn't stuck on anything.

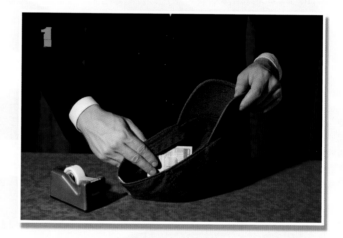

PERFORMANCE

1. Begin by asking a sports fan to volunteer from the audience. Then bring out the cards and name off the players. Lay the cards on the table as shown. Make sure the second identical card is the third card from your left. Next, ask the volunteer to choose a number between one and six.

Forced card

If they say, "One," start at your left and spell out O, N, E as shown.

If they say, "Two," start at your left and spell out T, W, O as shown.

If they say, "Three," start at your left and count 1, 2, 3 as shown.

If they say, "Four," start from your right and count 1, 2, 3, 4 as shown.

If they say, "Five," start at your right again and spell out F, I, V, E as shown.

If they say, "Six," start at your left and spell out S, I, X as shown.

2. When you land on the forced card, hold it up and tell the audience which one it is. Now, show the audience the foam finger. Say, "This magic finger can help me find the chosen card." Next, hold up the hat to show that it's empty. Be sure to cover the secret card with your hand as shown so the audience can't see it.

Secret card

3. Now, toss all the cards into the hat and shake them up a little. Don't shake too hard or the secret card might fall in with the rest of the cards. The trick will be ruined if this happens.

MAGIC TIP

When you count out the cards based on a chosen number, you will always land on the card you want. This is called "forcing" a card.

4. Next, put on the magic foam finger and dip it into the hat as shown. Make it fun for the audience by pretending to dig around inside the hat a little. You can even pretend that the finger gets stuck on something. When you're ready for the big finish, press the finger against the tape on the secret card so it sticks to the end.

5. Finally, slowly pull the foam finger out of the hat. Show the audience that the chosen card is magically stuck on the end. Say, "The magic finger never fails to find the card!" Then take a bow as the audience applauds!

SEE HOW IT'S DONE

THE CONFUSING COIN MYSTERY

Sometimes coins are found in the strangest places. This trick will stun your audience when extra coins magically appear in a volunteer's hands.

WHAT YOU NEED

- Eight coins
- An old book
- Scissors
- Glue

PREPARATION

1. First, make a secret pocket in the old book. Cut out a small space at the bottom of the book as shown. Make sure the pocket is big enough to fit two coins inside. Don't make it too big or the audience might see the hole.

2. To help keep the pages together, glue them around the secret pocket as shown. When the glue is dry, place two coins in the secret pocket.

MAGIC TIP

Always keep the secret pocket facing you so the audience and volunteer can't see the hole with the hidden coins.

1. Tell the audience a story about finding magical invisible coins in the air. Then place six coins on top of the book. Ask a volunteer to count the coins out loud with you. Then ask the volunteer to hold out his or her hands. Quickly tip the book so all the coins, including the hidden ones, slide into the volunteer's hands.

2. Tell the volunteer to hold the coins tightly. Then pretend to find two invisible coins in the air. Pretend to toss the coins through the book into the volunteer's hand. Ask, "Did you feel anything happen inside your hand?" The volunteer will probably say they didn't feel anything at all.

3. Finally, ask the volunteer to put the coins on the table and count them out loud again. The audience will be amazed when they see there are now eight coins. Thank the volunteer and ask the audience to give him or her a round of applause!

SEE HOW IT'S DONE

THE SPOOKY SPOON

Even ghosts like to go on picnics. Your friends will be spooked when this ghostly spoon disappears right before their eyes! With practice, you can make this simple trick look awesome!

WHAT YOU NEED

- A plastic spoon
- About 2 feet (0.6 meter) of thin elastic cord
- A safety pin
- A jacket with long sleeves
- An electric drill

PREPARATION

1. First, ask an adult to drill a small hole in the end of the spoon handle as shown. Then tie one end of the elastic thread through the hole in the spoon and the other end to the safety pin.

2. Next, connect the safety pin to the inside of your jacket at the collar. Then run the spoon and elastic down the inside of the jacket sleeve as shown.

1. Just before you do this trick, step off the stage or behind the curtain so the audience can't see you. Pull the spoon out of your sleeve and hold it in your hand as shown. Tell the audience a spooky story about the ghostly spoon. Say, "This spoon belongs to a ghost. Sometimes it takes the spoon back without any warning!"

2. Now, pretend to try and grab the spoon with both hands. As you do this, let go of the spoon.

3. When you let go of the spoon, let it slide back up your sleeve as shown.

4. Finally, open your hands and show the audience that the spoon has vanished into thin air. Say, "I guess the ghost was ready for his dinner and wanted his spoon back!"

THE MAGIC MATCHBOX BANK

You can save money without making a trip to the bank! Just sprinkle some magic dust and your coins travel to a safe place. This magical traveling penny will keep your audience in awe.

PREPARATION

1. Place one of the pennies between the inner and outer parts of the matchbox as shown. Make sure the penny is completely covered so the audience won't see it.

PERFORMANCE

1. First, show the audience that the matchbox is empty. Say, "I've found a new kind of savings bank." Then close the box so the secret penny slides into it and set it aside. Next, take out the second penny and show it to the audience.

SEE HOW IT'S DONE

22

Hidden penny

2. Now, hold the penny between your thumb and first finger. Then pretend to grab the penny with your other hand. But instead of grabbing it, you will drop it into your palm as shown. It looks like you're holding the coin in the second hand, but you are really hiding it in the palm of the first hand. This old trick is called the French Drop. Practice this move until it looks smooth and natural.

3. Now, reach into your pocket for some invisible magic dust with the hand holding the penny. Leave the penny in your pocket, then pretend to sprinkle magic dust over your empty hand.

4. Next, open your hands wide to show the audience that the penny has vanished!

5. Finally, open the matchbox and take out the secret penny. Show it to the audience. They will be stunned at how the penny magically traveled from your hand to the matchbox!

THE EGG-STRAORDINARY EGG

Are you ever in a hurry and don't have time for lunch? With this fun trick you can make an egg magically appear and cook it up fast. You'll leave the audience wondering how it's done!

WHAT YOU NEED

- ⭐ A hat
- ⭐ A handkerchief
- ⭐ A plastic egg
- ⭐ A plastic "cooked" egg
- ⭐ A plate
- ⭐ Thread
- ⭐ Clear tape

PREPARATION

1. First, measure and cut thread to fit between the edge and the center of the handkerchief. Then tape one end of the thread to the end of the plastic egg.

2. Attach the other end of the thread to the center of one side of the hanky. The plastic egg should be near the center of the hanky. Finally, put the plastic "cooked" egg into the hat.

SEE HOW IT'S DONE

1. First, tell the audience that you're feeling hungry. Say, "I think it's time for a snack." Then pick up the hat and show the audience that it's empty. When you pick it up, hide the "cooked" egg under your hand as shown. Then put the hat down and let the "cooked" egg drop into it.

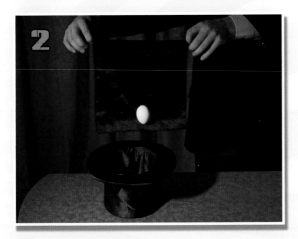

"Cooked" egg

2. Next, pick up the hanky by the corners as shown so the egg hangs behind it as shown. But be sure to do this with the egg facing you so the audience can't see it.

3. Now, fold the hanky in half with the egg inside. Hold it above the hat and say the magic words, "Cluck, Cluck, Cluck!" Then let the egg fall from the hanky into the hat.

4. Next, place the hanky over the hat and pretend to cook the egg with magic fire. Then raise the hanky up so the egg is lifted out of the hat. Toss the hanky and egg into your magic trunk. Finally, flip the hat over the plate and show the audience your delicious cooked egg!

THE AMAZING HEALING ROPE

Your audience will have a great time with this funny rope trick. They'll think you goofed at first. But they'll be stunned when the rope is magically healed right before their eyes!

WHAT YOU NEED

- ⭐ Two pieces of rope about 3 feet (1 m) long
- ⭐ Two or three pieces of rope about 4 inches (10 centimeters) long
- ⭐ Two large paper bags
- ⭐ Scissors
- ⭐ Tape

PREPARATION

1. First, cut one of the paper bags in half lengthwise as shown. Leave the bottom of the bag intact.

2. Tape the half bag inside the whole bag to make a secret pocket as shown.

3. Next, make a small loop about 1 foot (0.3 m) from the end of one of the long ropes. Tie a loose knot around the loop with one of the short rope pieces as shown above. The long rope should look like it has been cut and tied back together.

4. Now, tie one or two more knots in the same way onto the rope. Keep the knots about 1 foot (0.3 m) apart. The rope should now look similar to the picture.

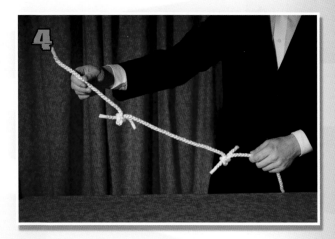

5. Place the knotted rope into the paper bag. Leave the secret pocket empty.

1. First, tell the audience that you have a trick that will astound them. Then show them the second long rope and say, "This amazing magic rope can heal itself if it's cut." Then hold up the rope and cut it into equal pieces.

2. Next, slide the pieces of rope into the secret pocket in the paper bag. Don't let the audience see the secret pocket!

3. Now, shake the bag around a little. Pretend that the pieces of rope are jumping around inside and are trying to heal themselves. You can also wave your magic wand over the bag as you do this.

4. Next, reach into the bag and pull out the knotted rope. Toss the bag out of sight. Say, "The rope is whole again! Isn't that amazing?" The audience will probably laugh when they see that the rope is just tied together. Try acting confused. But tell them that you can fix it. You just need a volunteer's help. Ask someone to help you fix the rope.

5. Ask the volunteer to blow on one of the knots. As he or she blows, pull the rope tight. The knot should pop right off the rope. Say, "Wow! You're better at this than I thought!"

6. Finally, ask the volunteer to blow on the other knot. Pull the rope tight so the other knots pop off like before. Show the magically healed rope to the audience. Thank the volunteer and ask him or her to take a bow while the audience gives you both a round of applause!

SEE HOW IT'S DONE

GLOSSARY

applause (uh-PLAWZ)—clapping hands to show appreciation or approval

audience (AW-dee-uhns)—people who watch or listen to a play, movie, or show

balance (BA-luhnts)—to keep steady and not fall over

force card (FORSS KARD)—a card that a magician tricks an audience into choosing

French Drop (FRENCH DROP)—an old method of secretly hiding a coin in the palm of the hand to make it seem that the coin has disappeared

identical (eye-DEN-ti-kuhl)—exactly alike

misdirection (mis-di-REK-shuhn)—a method of getting an audience to look the wrong way while the magician secretly does something else

prop (PROP)—an item used by an actor or performer during a show

trunk (TRUHNGK)—a large case or box used for storage or for carrying items

volunteer (vol-uhn-TIHR)—someone who offers to help perform a task during a show

READ MORE

Barnhart, Norm. *Stunning Stage Tricks.*
Magic Manuals. North Mankato, Minn.:
Capstone Press, 2014.

Hunter, Nick. *Fun Magic Tricks.* Try This at Home!
Chicago: Capstone Raintree, 2013.

Turnbull, Stephanie. *Easy Mind and Body Tricks.*
Beginner Magic. Mankato, Minn.: Smart Apple
Media, 2014.

· · · · · · ·

INTERNET SITES

Use FactHound to find Internet sites
related to this book.

Visit www.facthound.com

Just type in 9781543505719 and go.

Super-cool stuff! Check out projects, games and lots more at
www.capstonekids.com

INDEX

cards, 6–7, 10–11,
    14–17
coins, 6–7, 18–19,
    22–23

French Drop, 23

hankies, 24–25
hats, 14, 16–17, 24–25

magic trunks, 4, 7, 13, 25
magic wands, 7, 12–13, 28
magic words, 25
misdirection, 4

paper bags, 26–29
ping-pong balls, 12–13
practice, 4
props, 4

ropes, 26–29

secrets, 4, 5, 9, 10, 11,
    14–15, 16–17, 18,
    22–23, 26, 27, 28
spoons, 20–21
stories, 4, 9, 11, 12, 19, 21

volunteers, 14, 18, 19, 29